The Experience of LANDSCAPE

paintings, drawings and photographs from the Arts Council Collection

South Bank Centre 1987–89

Preface

During the last forty or fifty years, when changes in technology and society have been matched for pace by rapid and radical changes in art, landscape has continued to command the attention of a huge number of artists.

The Experience of Landscape is intended, not as a survey, but to show and compare the range of artists' responses to an almost equal variety of countryside, from the domestic seclusion of a Sussex garden to the furthest and wildest coasts of Scotland.

In this catalogue we have gathered an anthology of pictures from the exhibition with poems of the same period. We are grateful to many people, including artists, who have provided advice and information, and to those who have granted permission to publish poems. We thank, in particular, Jeremy Hooker whom we invited, as a poet, to write about the pictures in the exhibition, and to Jonathan Barker who has selected the poetry.

Joanna Drew
Director of Hayward and Regional Exhibitions

Michael Harrison
Assistant Director for Regional Exhibitions

The Experience of Landscape

painting and poetry

JEREMY HOOKER

There is, I think, an art of seeing that applies equally to pictures and to nature. It is a way of entering each attentively, and exploring what is there, and it enlarges the world, and induces a feeling of awe, which emphasises the bounds of one's knowledge and descriptive powers. It is an art which relates the person to the *other*, instead of reducing the *other* to the confines of the self. Thus, looking with delight at landscape art, as my mind and eye enter more fully into each composition, and at the same time recognise formal and thematic relationships among various works, I have an increasing sense of the limits of what can be said. As the Scottish poet Hugh MacDiarmid stood on a raised beach and felt, 'I look at these stones and know little about them', so I stand in front of David Bomberg's *Trendrine Cornwall* and know the poverty of my vocabulary of colour, or in front of Mary Potter's *Sun on the Beach* and know that words like symbol and impression simply miss the painting's effect. The same is true of my experience of nature, which the pictures influence. I grew up in a home that was full of landscape paintings, mainly of water, light and trees, in constant movement and change. These were as 'natural' to me as the places outside the home that had inspired them. In course of time, I saw more in the places because of the paintings, and more in the paintings by the light of nature. But to see more is both to value what is revealed, and to feel acutely the difficulty of doing justice to it with words.

'Landscape' is a concept that points in two directions, to the picture in the frame and to part of the world outside the frame, and therefore raises unavoidable questions about the relation between art and reality. This is not the place to analyse that relation in depth, and in any case I would rather celebrate transactions between the two meanings of 'landscape'. To simplify, as I must in a brief introduction, it seems to me reasonable to suppose that each of the artists represented in the exhibition, however proud or modest by temperament, first stood in front of a landscape and felt, like MacDiarmid, awed by something vastly greater than his or her knowledge. This supposition doesn't ignore the manifest differences between descriptive and visionary landscapes, as we see them in the window views of Charles Ginner and Winifred Nicholson, for example, or between different forms of abstraction, as in Brian Wynter's geometrical forms and Bomberg's painting, which calls to mind Van Gogh's prediction of an art 'closer to music, where colour would reign supreme'. Rather, it is based on the evidence of the pictures

7 DAVID BOMBERG *Trendrine, Cornwall*
1947
oil on canvas

4 FRANK AUERBACH *Primrose Hill, Summer Sunshine* 1964
oil on board

themselves, which shows that the artists have first experienced landscape, and that their work is an effort to attain further knowledge, whether through truth to impressions of the world or through non-descriptive elements. The Impressionist Alfred Sisley said, 'Every picture exhibits a place the artist has fallen in love with'. That has the vulnerability of all such general statements, but, as a description of landscape art, I like it very much, especially since love can take many different forms, and often includes or interacts with other, darker emotions.

Now, we are more inclined to look *at* pictures rather than *through* them, as if they were windows on their subjects. But although every real work of art is an object which makes creative use of its medium, I don't believe that a single one, from paleolithic cave paintings to the present day, exists *only* for its own sake. Art is a vision of the world, even if one describes it, less resonantly, as Emile Zola did, as 'a corner of nature seen through a temperament'. As far as the landscapes of Britain are concerned, artists such as Bomberg, Winifred Nicholson, Joan Eardley, and Michael Fussell do in their terms what Molly Holden does in her poem «In this unremarkable island» (p. 45): they surprise us with remarkable, beautiful and mysterious effects of weather and light. Molly Holden is writing in a great tradition of English poetry, which includes contemporary poets as well as Wordsworth and Clare and Hardy. It is a tradition that shares the spirit of Constable's gratitude to the banks of his native Stour for making him a painter, and, like him, finds its art 'under every hedge and in every lane'. Coleridge describes Wordsworth's object in his poems in *Lyrical Ballads* as, 'to give the charm of novelty to things of every day, and to excite a feeling analogous to the supernatural, by awakening the mind's attention to the lethargy of custom, and directing it to the loveliness and the wonders of the world before us'. He is speaking, like Constable, about an art of seeing, without which 'we have eyes, yet see not'. The experience of landscape art is, often, a seeing of common places and 'things of every day' for the first time.

Of course, it is not only a gentle beauty or mystery that artists disclose in unseen familiar places. Who would have thought Primrose Hill a place on fire with solar energy, where waves of red heat seem to break out of the ground? In Frank Auerbach's *Primrose Hill, Summer Sunshine* the paint looks trowelled on, gouged, handled with intense, even violent, yet sensitive feeling. It bears the marks of a struggle to convey a vision, which is what I value most in any art, and find, in different forms, in many works in this exhibition. And where better to show nature's solar and volcanic forces than in a place in which the eye dulled by 'the lethargy of custom' is least likely to see them? Auerbach, like Bomberg and Victor Pasmore and Roger Hilton, paints an 'active universe', but with a more dangerous energy than Wordsworth perceived. Every artist of worth sees things differently, with a personal vision. But what all see is truer than a literal photographic description to the nature we live in and are part of, whether their truth is to atmosphere, or to underlying structures, or to elemental forces. A Turner, a Palmer, a Pasmore abstraction, all reveal to us *our* world: the world in which we really find ourselves, rather than the world we may think we possess. Long ago, I learnt from Paul Nash to see truths about downland that I would not have seen otherwise. Of course, without his work, I would have missed his vision. But Nash's art of seeing reveals correspondences between different objects and scales and forces that are actually there, in the life of the subject. Landscape art is a personal, partial revelation of nature. It enlarges and subtilizes our sense of a world in which, in the words of R.S. Thomas's «The View from the Window» (p. 68), 'colours/Are renewed daily with variations/Of light and distance', there is constant movement and change, and creation is at work on a painting that is never the same but always finished.

What does Winifred Nicholson reveal in her *Cumberland Hills*? Purple orchids in a vase at a window that opens on a view of azure uplands. Her medium is paint, but I have to revert to the language of music or poetry to suggest what she shows. Green leaves echo a green, globular vase, which in colour and shape echoes fields below the hills. Curtains and distant uplands are like forms made of the same light and air. It is a wonderfully fresh, delicate painting, which unites the near and the far, the inner and outer worlds, and discloses a harmony of plant, earth and sky. *Cumberland Hills* shows in manmade and natural objects the one sensitive life. Looking at it, I could see why the poet Frances Horovitz loved Winifred Nicholson's paintings.

In her poem «Walking in Autumn» (p. 40), Frances Horovitz images treading on fallen crab apples, 'feet crunching into mud/the hard slippery yellow moons'. The image identifying apple and moon, heavenly body and earthly fruit, calls to mind the sun and moon images, and other images connecting different elements, that haunt a

opposite
54 WINIFRED NICHOLSON
Cumberland Hills 1948
oil on wood

below
57 MARY POTTER *Sun on the Beach*
1961
oil on canvas

number of the pictures. Paul Nash has been called 'Master of the image', and in *Nest of Wild Stones*, with its pebbles shaped like eggs or astronomical spheres, and flints which might also be Avebury sarsens, and are like skylarks, one can see why. He animates the inanimate, relates different scales in nature, and earth and sky, and his images are presences, charged with numinous power. This is a consciously symbolic art, which rearranges things in order to intimate the reality behind appearances, and it may usefully be called poetic. But although I am tempted to use literary terms in describing some other works, they seem merely clumsy when applied to Winifred Nicholson's painting, or to the thistledown sun in Joan Eardley's beautiful *A Field of Oats*, or to Mary Potter's *Sun on the Beach*. Nevertheless, it is not only what Charles Tomlinson calls 'a language of water, light and air' (p. 73) that landscape artists, like poets, seek, but also presences, or images that make the *other* present.

Sun on the Beach is a haunting painting of light and of contrasting, interacting objects and elements. The yellow sun is as much on the beach as a ball might be, and the boat, a pale curved shape linking beach and sea, is like a moon. The correspondence of sun and moon-boat is elusive, unselfconscious; I tried applying to it the word symbol but the picture rejected it. But this is not *only* a painting of things in sunlight. The winter shrub in the sea-garden has a spikiness (with just a hint of a Sutherland-like crown of thorns) and the objects on the beach a raggedness, which contrast with the smooth lines of beach and wall. A balance of opposing forces, light and dark, sun and moon, earth and sea, the enclosed world of room and garden and the unenclosed outer world, is implicit in the vision. Like sun and shrub and moon-boat, the strange, pale faces of cabbages in the seagarden are presences.

In other pictures, trees have an equivalent life. Robert Colquhoun's *Church Lench* is a wartime landscape. The shapes and dark green of tree crowns and trunks hold a tension between peaceful stillness and menace. There is a 'dark' feeling, which the one white tree intensifies, and reveals its cause as the threat of death. Something of the many different languages that trees are capable of providing may be seen, also, in the photographs by Paul Nash, the drawings by David Nash, and Elisabeth Vellacott's *Winter Trees*. Looking at David Jones's *Tree Trunks and Shed*, one might know nothing of his religious and mythological concerns, and still, in the stature and centrality of the foreground tree, in its reaching up and out, and above all in its sensitive organic being, see an image of the Tree of Life.

'I should paint my own places best—Painting is but another word for feeling.' Yes. But Constable's self-prescription is patently not applicable to many artists, who find places to fall in love with away from home, whether in Cornwall or Provence or Andalusia or Skye, and make them their own. It is a paradox familiar to me from poems of place that the art of seeing often involves, in some sense, distance from the place seen. On the one hand, I think of Richard Jefferies's statement that in order to know a place, 'It is necessary to stay in it like the oaks'. And on the other, of the figure in W.H. Auden's *The Wanderer*, 'a stranger to strangers over undried sea', who dreams of home, and wakes to see nameless birds, and people making 'another love'. It is not only that at least some distance is necessary before one can see anything at all, but that a degree of estrangement renews the world, and may transfigure it. The artist is inward with the otherness of landscape, but often experiences it as a wanderer, bringing to it needs and feelings born of the distance between the human and the natural world. A dream of home pervades many British landscapes, in paintings and poems, and may express desire for one or several things: Paradise, Eden, a return to personal or cultural origins, union with the beloved or with nature, death. Coleridge links the aim of giving 'the charm of novelty to things of every day' and the aim of exciting 'a feeling analogous to the supernatural'. Indeed, there are few good landscapes in which one can separate the aims completely, or make a rigid distinction between an atmosphere arising from intimacy with the place, and an atmosphere expressing the vision of a wanderer or dreamer. Thus Michael Fussell, in *Heavy Rain over a Marsh (Winter Rain)*, uses curving strokes of charcoal with deceptive simplicity, expressing both the essence of weather and place, and a visionary mood. Ivon Hitchens, in another work rich in atmosphere, paints a leafy, watery otherworld in his *Garden Cove*. He succeeds in depicting England as an enchanted realm, because his vision is not based on cerebral fantasy, but rooted in physical, sensuous experience. His otherworld is, also, Sussex. In Sargy Mann's *River Box*, too, the place has been lived in, known from the inside, its conditions weathered; but it is not only natural knowledge arising from being in a place like an oak that shines in the glint of water and the tiny candleflame of sunlight, which lead deep into the formidable, dark mass of vegetation.

11 ROBERT COLQUHOUN *Church Lench*
1942
oil on canvas

19 W G GILLIES *Eildon* 1949
oil on canvas

42 SIR WILLIAM MACTAGGART
Winter Sunset, the Red Soil 1956
oil on canvas

Responding to personal and cultural need, a number of the best modern British poets evoke presences in the landscape and landscapes charged with power, and, like the artists, they frequently use imagery of light and dark. They summon up the historical past and the life of nature, or they project a lost religion or integration onto landscape. David Jones in «The Sleeping Lord» (p. 30) identifies potent elements of Welsh history and myth with 'the configuration of the land' itself. Landscape paintings may have an equivalent charge, in images and symbols, and perhaps above all in rhythmic movements of lines, colours and shapes. The artists don't exactly show 'history' as poets, let alone historians, treat it, but rather long-inhabited places, in which the relationship between man and the land is strongly defined. Sir William MacTaggart's *Winter Sunset, the Red Soil* (a title that is an imagist poem) is a painting whose dynamic rhythmic movements charge it with energy and meaning. Red sun and red-brown earth, irregular curved shapes of sun and trees and fields, all move in relation to one another, and man's place in nature, his home among solar and earthly powers, is implicit in the house with its red-brown roof. By contrast, Sheila Fell's *Woman in the Snow* conceives the human on a more heroic scale. Here, corresponding sombre colours and massy forms relate the woman's capacity for strength and endurance to the buildings'. Unlike the enigmatic and disquieting human presence in Carel Weight's work, the woman has a dependable solidity, and is more like a Tolstoyan peasant than one of Hardy's figures, 'slighted and enduring'. Absence, too, can be a kind of presence, in pictures in which the external world is depicted with loving attentiveness, as if the artist, like C.H. Sisson in his poem «Burrington Combe» (p. 34), has revealed place as it is without him, or as in the loneliness that haunts L.S. Lowry's flat, blue-grey, empty *Seascape*.

Descriptive paintings, like Charles Ginner's *The Window* and Leonard Appelbee's *Barns in a Field,* may remind us that landscape, which is itself an artefact, can seem to create its own abstractions by juxtaposing different objects with similar shapes. Indeed, different landscapes have different rhythms. I mean by this something more than the Classical concept of *genius loci*, or spirit of place, although this is part of it. The rhythms express a total environment: geological structure, soil type, native vegetation and wild life, effects of human occupation and labour, and also cultural significance, its symbolic shape in the imagination of a people. I don't mean that anyone sees all this, but that an artist, without deriving his art naively from them, may be most indebted to wild or cultivated landscape for a sense of its rhythms. For example, in Roger Hilton's *January 1964, Red*, in which the abstraction arises from a Cornish landscape of cliffs and mines, and from forms such as shells and the female body, and in Brian Wynter's *Landscape, Zennor*, we may see the relationship between perceived rhythms and abstract form. Victor Pasmore's *The Snowstorm: Spiral Motif in Black and White* reveals a similar, but more immaterial transaction between the imagination and the elements. The transaction is as old as the art of the caves, and it reveals not only a delight in creating formal patterns but the forces that create, destroy, and continue life.

The art of seeing petrifies, if it is not continually renewed. At first, I looked over rather than at Robert Law's *The White Horse of Uffington*, because it did not match the image of the original fixed in my mind. But how could it? The white horse, an image that is part of the land itself, and moves with its rhythms, is the most dynamic manmade work in these islands. But of course, Robert Law isn't competing with his subject. Looking again at his drawing, I saw that the words at the top are an integral part of the image: 'ACROSS THE WAVING CORN PAST THE LOOKOUT POST TO THE WHITE HORSE OF UFFINGTON CASTLE'. Artist and viewer both *look across* the waving corn, but both also, in a sense, *approach* the figure, crossing the space bodily, over a distance evoked by drawing and words. The distance is physical, but the childlike waving corn and skeletal horse, like slivers of picked bone, also mark a temporal distance, between the primitive and the modern, and between child and adult artist. Or perhaps they mark the distance only to annul it, and unite past and present, child and man, rather as certain modern poets, such as David Jones and Seamus Heaney, return to personal and cultural origins. Another 'primitive' work, W.G. Gillies's *Eildon*—its dark green the colour both of our sombre northern wilderness and of the primordial vegetative world—also establishes a relationship between child's eye and artist's eye. In the horses that crop the grass, yet look like hill-cut figures, and in the bold, simplifying, suggestive lines in which hillshapes, horsebacks and beehive ricks echo one another, a connection is made, as in the Law, between the age of the hills and the individual human lifespan, and between the innocent eye and adult experience.

The words at the bottom of Hamish Fulton's *Seven days Alberta* are as much part of the image as Law's words are part of his drawing. In

8 MARK BOYLE and JOAN HILLS
Bonfire Study 1976
coal, burnt wood, stones, ash and scorched earth on fibre glass

Fulton's work, they underline the experience of finding the sticks in the Rocky Mountains and thus reinforce the authority of the artist, who has also arranged and photographed them. This is a sophisticated, selfconscious, actively imaginative form of 'found' art. Together with several other works, David Nash's *Larch framed with Larch* and *Ash framed with Ash*, Mark Boyle's *Bonfire Study*, John Latham's *Carberry Bing* and Terry Setch's *Penarth III*, it reminded me of William Carlos Williams's famous poetic prescription: 'no ideas but in things'. Fortunately, the words are capable of several interpretations at least as various as these works. Thus, in the Terry Setch, the use of hot wax and oil paint creates an effect of the artist handling the actual substances of place—the clay, sand and pink stone of Penarth cliffs and beach. I have had an analogous sense, in writing poems about place, of working not only with words, but with the materials that the words name—chalk and flint, or shingle, mud, tar and salt water. John Latham's 'documentation', a photomontage which incorporates a jar of slagheap material, is a different treatment of the thing itself, although, as a celebration of the beauty that may be found in industrial waste, it also has something in common with William Scott's *Slagheap Landscape*, and, as an arrangement of multiple images, with John Virtue's atmospheric *Green Haworth*.

If Peter Lanyon's *Soaring Flight*, a beautiful, rhythmic painting of the sky seen from the sky, provides the least earthbound experience of landscape, it is difficult to imagine anything literally grittier or more down to earth than Mark Boyle's *Bonfire Study*. Here, it seems, is the very stuff of an actual place, just as it was in situ: 'coal, burnt wood, stones, ash and scorched earth' (and was the hayseed I saw clinging to it meant to be there?). But of course, this is not the debris of a bonfire but a bonfire *study*, in which the artist has used a fibreglass base, a secret method of composition, and substances already shaped or affected by human agency, and found a new way to play imaginatively with the relation between realism and abstraction, and art and nature. In that respect, as in some others, *Bonfire Study* is not different in kind from other works in the exhibition. For landscape art is by definition a transaction with reality, and experience of it opens our eyes both to the world of the picture and the world outside it. Some of the artists are drawn to wild places, remote from what Edward Thomas called 'the parochialism of humanity', and others to the measured and manmade. But all bring us down to earth: to mystery, or the novelty of 'things of every day', or fiery energies burning in common places. They reveal or transform their experience in acts of personal vision, and disclose an art of seeing landscapes both in and out of the frame.

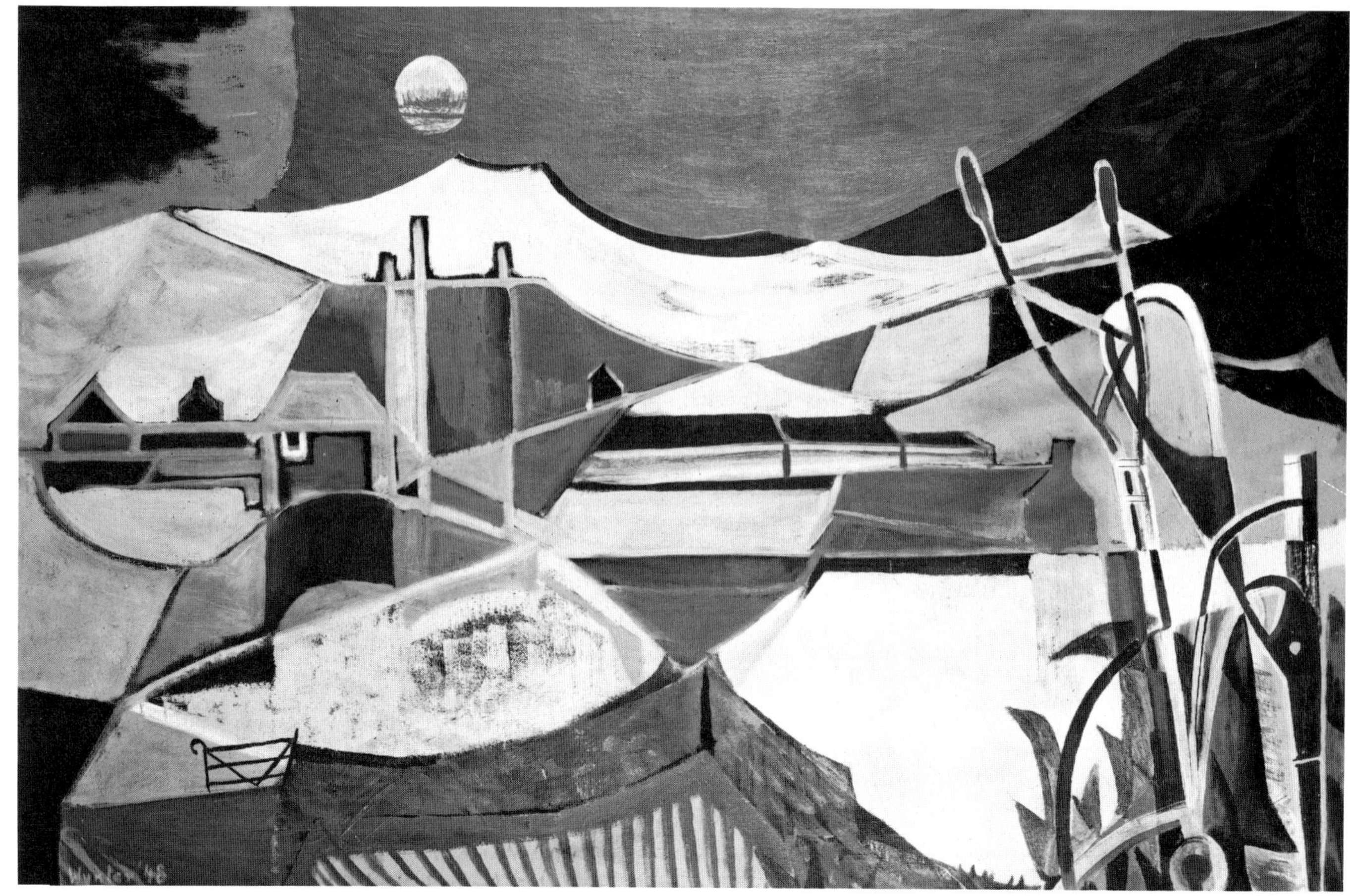

68 BRYAN WYNTER
Landscape, Zennor 1948
gouache on canvas

35 PETER LANYON
Moor Cliff, Kynance 1953
oil on board

5 WILHELMINA BARNS-GRAHAM
Grindelwald Glacier 1950
oil on canvas

ANNE STEVENSON

Walking Early by the Wye

Through dawn in February's wincing radiance.
Every splinter of river mist
rayed in my eyes.

As if the squint of the sun had released light's
metals. As if the river pulsed white,
and the holly's

sharp green lacquered leaves leaped acetylene.
As if the air smouldered from the ice of dry
pain, as if day

were fragmented in doubt. As if it were given
to enter alive the braided rings Saturn
is known by

and yet be allied to the dyke's heaped mud.
I will not forget how the ash trees stood,
silvered and still,

how each soft stone on its near shadow knelt,
how the sheep became stones where they built
their pearled hill.

Minute by Glass Minute Oxford University Press 1982

JEREMY HOOKER

from
Soliloquies of a Chalk Giant

I was with the first inhabitant
In these hills and I stayed here
After him, at the foot of his grave.

MATRIX

A memorial of its origins, chalk in barns and churches moulders in rain and damp; petrified creatures swim in its depths.

It is domestic, with the homeliness of an ancient hearth exposed to the weather, pale with the ash of countless primeval fires. Here the plough grates on an urnfield, the green plover stands with crest erect on a royal mound.

Chalk is the moon's stone; the skeleton is native to its soil. It looks anaemic, but has submerged the type-sites of successive cultures. Stone, bronze, iron: all are assimilated to its nature; and the hill-forts follow its curves.

These, surely, are the work of giants: temples rededicated to the sky god, spires fashioned for the lords of bowmen:

Spoils of the worn idol, squat Venus of the mines.

Druids leave their shops at the midsummer solstice; neophytes tread an antic measure to the antlered god. Men who trespass are soon absorbed, horns laid beside them in the ground. The burnt-out tank waits beside the barrow.

The god is a graffito carved on the belly of the chalk, his savage gesture subdued by the stuff of his creation. He is taken up like a gaunt white doll by the round hills, wrapped around by the long pale hair of the fields.

A View from the Source: Selected Poems Carcanet Press 1982

PHILIP PACEY

Charged Landscape: Uffington

From the eye of the Uffington White Horse
the downs' every feature. Spur, combe
and fluting; lifted by low sun

waves of a fossil sea, surging again
as wind through barley, breaking
on Berkshire's plain. The hand of man

who cleared scrub – yew and juniper; felled
trees below, exposing to view this land's
form, kept cropped by sheep and cultivation.

Cut through turf then, to this sea-horse,
tip of a contour's whip uncoiling,
crack of it – hoove's strike on storm's iron? –

lightning, will loose on earth rain.
At night, the white chalk reflecting, become
moon in the form, mare; fecund

to the sun her stallion. Who depended
for life on these things, each year
came as grooms to her, with hands scarred

by labour scouring flanks of the hill
until, the work done, made celebration in
the scooped hollow its earthen castle.

Come now, from close-to join up
detail to detail, bold
curve of back or foreleg, to an imagined

whole; and, from this eye, look to
the horizon, Harwell's shimmering:
charged with the same power that's here?

Charged Landscapes Enitharmon Press 1970

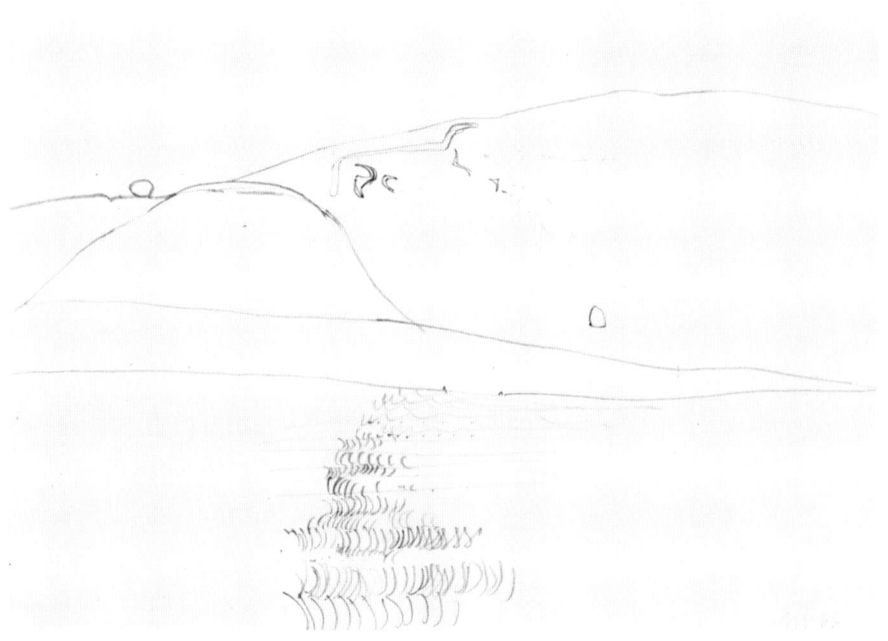

38 ROBERT LAW *Landscape Drawing, The White Horse of Uffington* 1966 pencil on paper

53 PAUL NASH *The White Horse, Uffington, Berkshire* c.1937 photograph, modern gelatin silver print

21 FAY GODWIN
Snow on desert of Wales 1976
photograph, gelatin silver print

67 CHRISTOPHER WOOD
Westmorland Landscape
pencil on paper

24 PAUL HILL *Stone Wall Complex, Under Whitle* 1981
photograph, gelatin silver print

FRANCES BELLERBY

Voices

I heard those voices today again:
Voices of women and children, down in that hollow
Of blazing light into which swoops the tree-darkened lane
Before it mounts up into the shadow again.

I turned the bend—just as always before
There was no one at all down there in the sunlit hollow;
Only ferns in the wall, foxgloves by the hanging door
Of that blind old desolate cottage. And just as before

I noticed the leaping glitter of light
Where the stream runs under the lane; in that mine-dark archway
—Water and stones unseen as though in the gloom of night—
Like glittering fish slithers and leaps the light.

I waited long at the bend of the lane,
But heard only the murmuring water under the archway.
Yet I tell you, I've been to that place again and again,

And always, in summer weather, those voices are plain,
Down near that broken house, just where the tree-darkened lane
Swoops into the hollow of light before mounting to shadow again.

Selected Poems Enitharmon Press 1986

TED HUGHES

Wodwo

What am I? Nosing here, turning leaves over
Following a faint stain on the air to the river's edge
I enter water. What am I to split
The glassy grain of water looking upward I see the bed
Of the river above me upside down very clear
What am I doing here in mid-air? Why do I find
this frog so interesting as I inspect its most secret
interior and make it my own? Do these weeds
know me and name me to each other have they
seen me before, do I fit in their world? I seem
separate from the ground and not rooted but dropped
out of nothing casually I've no threads
fastening me to anything I can go anywhere
I seem to have been given the freedom
of this place what am I then? And picking
bits of bark off this rotten stump gives me
no pleasure and it's no use so why do I do it
me and doing that have coincided very queerly
But what shall I be called am I the first
have I an owner what shape am I what
shape am I am I huge if I go
to the end on this way past these trees and past these trees
till I get tired that's touching one wall of me
for the moment if I sit still how everything
stops to watch me I suppose I am the exact centre
but there's all this what is it roots
roots roots roots and here's the water
again very queer but I'll go on looking

Wodwo Faber & Faber 1967

DAVID JONES

from The Sleeping Lord

Yet he sleeps on
very deep is his slumber:
how long has he been the sleeping lord?
are the clammy ferns
his rustling vallance
does the buried rowan
ward him from evil, or
does he ward the tanglewood
and the denizens of the wood
are the stunted oaks his gnarled guard
or are their knarred limbs
strong with his sap?
Do the small black horses
grass on the hunch of his shoulders?
are the hills his couch
or is he the couchant hills?
Are the slumbering valleys
him in slumber
are the still undulations
the still limbs of him sleeping?
Is the configuration of the land
the furrowed body of the lord
are the scarred ridges
his dented greaves
do the trickling gullies
yet drain his hog-wounds?
Does the land wait the sleeping lord
or is the wasted land
that very lord who sleeps?

The Sleeping Lord and other fragments Faber & Faber 1974

12 THOMAS JOSHUA COOPER *Ritual Indication, Nesscliffe, Shropshire*
1974
photograph, gelatin silver print

3 LEONARD APPELBEE *Barns in a field*
1940
oil on canvas

28 NICHOLAS HORSFIELD *River Epte* 1974
oil on canvas

43 SARGY MANN *River Box, evening Sun* 1981
oil on wood

C H SISSON

from **Burrington Combe**

When I walk out there will be nothing missing
That I can see;
The pond will be there with its fish,
The rosemary

Spreading itself over the garden
As if still aided by my hand;
The mulberry-tree I planted, and the cherry,
The old apple-trees and

The plums stretching up against the wall
Over which the church-tower still looks;
Starlings and swallows, the swans flying over,
And always the rooks.

And that distance into which I shall have vanished
Will still be there;
It was always dear to me, is now
In the thickening air.

No distance was ever like this one
The flat land with its willows, and the great sky
With the river reflecting its uncertainty
But no more I.

Collected Poems 1943–83 Carcanet Press 1984

RUTH PITTER

A Dream

This is a strange twilit country, but full of peace.
Faintly I hear sorrow; she sighs, moving away.
She goes, and guilt goes with her; all is forgiven.
Grey wolds and a slow dark river spell release
In this place where it is never quite night or day,
More like the elysian fields than the fields of heaven;

And no one here but I and this silent child.
She needs to sleep, I will carry her through the dim
Levels of this long river's deliberate mazes.
Nothing of man's is here, and never a wild
Creature to crop the grass or tunnel the brim
Of the full stream, or look up in our two faces.

She spoke so strangely that once, but she speaks no more.
Leans her head down in my neck, and is light to bear.
I think she walked here over the twilit stream.
I must find the tree, the elm by the river-shore,
Loosen her little arms and leave her there,
Under the boughs of sleep and the leaves of dream.

Poems 1926–1966 The Cresset Press 1968

PAUL HYLAND

Purbeck Progress

Salt mists creep on the sunlit hills
as if the sea beyond reclaimed
its own pure chalk whose calcined bone
under cropped grass is Purbeck's spine,
ocean's upswelling laid-down dead.

Below are clay-scapes, gravel troughs,
relicts of repetitious seas'
transgressions and retreats; the waste
acidic heath whose flagrant furze
like yeast, works in the sun's oven.

Furrows, like ripples in the rough,
struggle from farmsteads, and revert.
Seawards, ramparts raised on the chalk,
strip-lynchets, stones chart human tides
while mounds like sea-marks compass them.

Those barrows of trussed bones disperse
in mist up on the chilling ridge.
The humming heath lies undisturbed;
men settled on the sun-baked earth
that soon must break over their heads.

The Stubborn Forest Bloodaxe Books 1984

opposite
41 L S LOWRY *Seascape* 1965
oil on panel

below
47 RAYMOND MOORE *Maryport* 1977
photograph, gelatin silver print

40 JOHN LESSORE *La Gardie* 1964
oil on board

66 DERWENT WISE
Northumbrian Landscape 1975
acrylic on board

FRANCES HOROVITZ

Walking in Autumn

(for Diana Lodge)

We have overshot the wood.
The track has led us beyond trees
to the tarmac edge. Too late now
at dusk to return a different way,
hazarding barbed wire or an unknown bull.
We turn back onto the darkening path.
Pale under-leaves of whitebeam, alder
gleam at our feet like stranded fish
or Hansel's stones.
A wren, unseen, churrs alarm:
each tree drains to blackness.
Halfway now, we know
by the leaning crab-apple;
feet crunching into mud
the hard slippery yellow moons.
We hurry without reason
stumbling over roots and stones.
A night creature lurches, cries out,
crashes through brambles.
Skin shrinks inside our clothes;
almost we run
falling through darkness to the wood's end,
the gate into the sloping field.
Home is lights and woodsmoke, voices—
and, our breath caught, not trembling now,
a strange reluctance to enter within doors.

Collected Poems Bloodaxe Books: Enitharmon Press 1985

15 JOAN EARDLEY *A Field of Oats* 1962
oil on board

left
63 JOHN VIRTUE *Green Haworth I*
1979–80
pencil, charcoal and ink on paper

opposite
50 PAUL NASH *Night Landscape*
1912–14
watercolour and ink on paper

64 ANDREW WALTON
Garden at Night—Poles 1982
charcoal on paper

MOLLY HOLDEN

In this unremarkable island

We are always surprised by our weathers.

A morning sky is calm and apparently settled.
We assume a fine day to come. But clouds,
fine and soft, and ruffed like a comma's wings,
appear like phantoms in the distant blue.
We pay them little attention—perhaps they are
only signs of September at its best, a mellow sun
and the grass thicker with dew and shadow
than in these last few months.

But I
know what they mean; I am not surprised
by our weathers because I have had, perforce,
to sit and watch them change and come and go,
over the church or the chestnut, for nine years now.
I know the patterns of the sky and what they portend!
So now I watch a faint dappling in the west appear,
without surprise, and then, from nowhere apparently,
smooth pale banks of long and elegant cloud
behind those ragged wings that seemed diaphanous
at first but now become solid and significant.
I know that there will follow clouds scaled and veined,
and mares' tails twisted like ferns by winds at
incredible heights, and of incredibly cold
crystal, to such a coil of pattern
that no Celtic silversmith could match,
for all his skill. All this to herald rain!

Now, are we not spoilt, to live with such skies?
Although, soon after them, the sheet of faceless cloud
will move in on us from the west, drop,
silently drizzle, I would not live otherwhere.

They do not have such skies even in Calabria.

Selected Poems Carcanet Press 1987

NORMAN NICHOLSON

Cloud on Black Combe

The air clarifies. Rain
Has clocked off for the day.

The wind scolds in from Sligo,
Ripping the calico-grey from a pale sky.
Black Combe holds tight
To its tuft of cloud, but over the three-legged island
All the west is shining.

An hour goes by,
And now the starched collars of the eastern pikes
Streak up into a rinse of blue. Every
Inland fell is glinting;
Black Combe alone still hides
Its bald, bleak forehead, balaclava'd out of sight.

Slick fingers of wind
Tease and fidget at wool-end and wisp,
Picking the mist to bits.
Strings and whiskers
Fray off from the cleft hill's
Bilberried brow, disintegrate, dissolve
Into blue liquidity—
Only a matter of time
Before the white is wholly worried away
And Black Combe starts to earn its name again.

Sea to the West Faber & Faber 1981

NORMAN MACCAIG

In a Mist

The mountains fold and move.
I'm not quite lost. The thing that troubles me
Is that the easiest way out
Is not the one that's easiest to see.

I know just where you are.
But how to get there when lochs change their place
And the familiar track
Squirms like an adder into the heather bushes?

I curse my senses: and speak
Into the mist: Stay where you are, please stay –
I've got my compass yet.
It'll get me to you, if not by the easiest way.

Collected Poems Chatto and Windus/Hogarth Press 1985

30 JOHN DICKSON INNES *Arenig* 1911
watercolour on paper

14 JOHN A DAVIES
Wicklow Mountains, Wicklow 1981
photograph, gelatin silver print

18 MICHAEL FUSSELL *Heavy Rain over a Marsh (Winter Rain)* 1959
charcoal on paper

2 NORMAN ADAMS *Study of the Sun—Evening, Staffin Bay, Skye* 1965
watercolour and pencil on paper

36 PETER LANYON *Soaring Flight* 1960
oil on canvas

MICHAEL HAMBURGER

Oak

Slow in growth, late in putting out leaves,
And the full leaves dark, austere,
Neither the flower nor the fruit sweet
Save to the harsh jay's tongue, squirrel's and boar's,
Oak has an earthward urge, each bough dithers,
Now rising, now jerked aside, twisted back,
Only the bulk of the lower trunk keeps
A straight course, only the massed foliage together
Rounds a shape out of knots and zigzags.

But when other trees, even the late-leaved ash,
Slow-growing walnut, wide-branching beech and linden
Sway in a summer wind, poplar and willow bend,
Oak alone looks compact, in a stillness hides
Black stumps of limbs that blight or blast bared;
And for death reserves its more durable substance.
On wide floorboards four centuries old,
Sloping, yet scarcely worn, I can walk
And in words not oaken, those of my time, diminished,
Mark them that never were a monument
But plain utility, and mark the diminution,
Loss of that patient tree, loss of the skills
That matched the patience, shaping hard wood
To outlast the worker and outlast the user;
How by oak beams, worm-eaten,
This cottage stands, when brick and plaster have crumbled,
In casements of oak the leaded panes rest
Where new frames, new doors, mere deal, again and again have rotted.

PHILIP LARKIN

The Trees

The trees are coming into leaf
Like something almost being said;
The recent buds relax and spread,
Their greenness is a kind of grief.

Is it that they are born again
And we grow old? No, they die too.
Their yearly trick of looking new
Is written down in rings of grain.

Yet still the unresting castles thresh
In fullgrown thickness every May.
Last year is dead, they seem to say,
Begin afresh, afresh, afresh.

High Windows Faber & Faber 1974

ANDREW YOUNG

The Beech-Wood

When the long, varnished buds of beech
Point out beyond their reach,
And tanned by summer suns
Leaves of black bryony turn bronze,
And gossamer floats bright and wet
From trees that are their own sunset,
Spring, summer, autumn I come here,
And what is there to fear?
And yet I never lose the feeling
That someone close behind is stealing
Or else in front has disappeared;
Though nothing I have seen or heard,
The fear of what I might have met
Makes me still walk beneath these boughs
With cautious step as in a haunted house.

The Poetical Works of Andrew Young ed. with an introduction and notes by Edward Lowbury and Alison Young Secker & Warburg 1985

55 VICTOR PASMORE *Riverside Gardens, Hammersmith* c.1944
oil on canvas

32 DAVID JONES
Tree Trunks and Shed 1948
watercolour and pencil on paper

David Jones
Feb + March 48

opposite
49 DAVID NASH
Larch framed with Larch 1978
charcoal on paper with larch frame

right
52 PAUL NASH
Dead Tree, Romney Marsh c.1937
photograph, modern gelatin silver print

opposite
6 ELINOR BELLINGHAM-SMITH
Winter Afternoon 1952
oil on canvas

below
62 ELISABETH VELLACOTT
Winter Trees 1969
pencil on paper

SEVEN DAYS

WHISTLING ELK

A SEVEN DAY WALK IN THE ROCKY MOUNTAINS OF ALBERTA

CANADA AUTUMN 1978

17 HAMISH FULTON
Seven Days Alberta 1978
sepia toned photograph and letraset text on card

46 JOHN MINTON
Surrey Landscape 1944
pen and ink and wash on paper

CHARLES CAUSLEY

Who?

Who is that child I see wandering, wandering
Down by the side of the quivering stream?
Why does he seem not to hear, though I call to him?
Where does he come from, and what is his name?

Why do I see him at sunrise and sunset
Taking, in old-fashioned clothes, the same track?
Why, when he walks, does he cast not a shadow
Though the sun rises and falls at his back?

Why does the dust lie so thick on the hedgerow
By the great field where a horse pulls the plough?
Why do I see only meadows, where houses
Stand in a line by the riverside now?

Why does he move like a wraith by the water,
Soft as the thistledown on the breeze blown?
When I draw near him so that I may hear him,
Why does he say that his name is my own?

Collected Poems 1951–1975 Macmillan 1975

ROBERT WELLS

'The Wind Blows'

The wind blows. Winds blow the
Hill green and grey. Olives
Are alive with light. Fat grow the
Grapes green-misted with a mist that lives.

I wait living with these things by the lake.
My eyelids poise over my eyes. Closing
To kill sight they hover in the wake
Of the crowd of things their uncovering unclosed –

Where over the lake two hawks poise and hover.
Intention tips their wings like light.
When the wake of the boat uncovers
Fish tossed out dead they arch their flight.

Selected Poems Carcanet Press 1986

THOMAS A. CLARK

as I walked out early
into the order of things
the world was up before me
as I stepped out bravely
the very camber of the road
turned me to its purpose
it was on a morning early
I put design behind me
hear us and deliver us
to the hazard of the road
in all the anonymous places
where the couch grass grows
watch over us and keep us
to the temper of the road

Sixteen Sonnets Moschatel Press 1981

16 SHEILA FELL
Woman in the Snow 1955
oil on canvas

opposite
9 BILL BRANDT
Pilgrims' Way, Kent 1950
photograph, silver bromide print

below
65 CAREL WEIGHT
The Good Samaritan 1958
oil on canvas

61 SIR MATTHEW SMITH
Provençal Landscape c.1935
oil on canvas

44 BERNARD MENINSKY
Andalusian Landscape c.1936
oil on canvas

GEOFFREY GRIGSON

A Bright Decay

This side of the window glass
A bending stem holds up
A weakening flower.
How do I say

The red colour of a weakening flower?

Outside the window glass,
The late snow falling, the falling
Hypnotizing snow, the falling
Falling snow, this side

The red colour of a weakening flower?

The Fiesta Secker and Warburg 1978

R. S. THOMAS

The View from the Window

Like a painting it is set before one,
But less brittle, ageless; these colours
Are renewed daily with variations
Of light and distance that no painter
Achieves or suggests. Then there is movement,
Change, as slowly the cloud bruises
Are healed by sunlight, or snow caps
A black mood; but gold at evening
To cheer the heart. All through history
The great brush has not rested,
Nor the paint dried; yet what eye,
Looking coolly, or, as we now,
Through the tears' lenses, ever saw
This work and it was not finished?

Selected Poems 1946–1968 Bloodaxe Books 1986

LOUIS MACNIECE

Snow

The room was suddenly rich and the great bay-window was
Spawning snow and pink roses against it
Soundlessly collateral and incompatible:
World is suddener than we fancy it.

World is crazier and more of it than we think,
Incorrigibly plural. I peel and portion
A tangerine and spit the pips and feel
The drunkenness of things being various.

And the fire flames with a bubbling sound for world
Is more spiteful and gay than one supposes—
On the tongue on the eyes on the ears in the palms of one's
hands—
There is more than glass between the snow and the huge roses.

Collected Poems ed. E. R. Dodds Faber & Faber 1966

left
20 CHARLES GINNER
Spring Day at Boscastle 1943
oil on canvas

opposite
23 DUNCAN GRANT *The Doorway* 1929
oil on canvas

GEORGE BARKER

The great gales rage in the trees

The great gales rage in the trees outside the window.
      The moon races
over mottled water meadows and in shadows
      and moonlight the surfaces
      of the nightmare stream glint
and shiver in the wind as winter
      shrieks in the chimney stack
and not even the far obedient star
      believes it can ever bring
      the summer back.
The dog whimpers. A door slams. The shutters
      clap and a sleeping child
      stirs with a haunted sigh
      as the storm mutters
and groans around this dreaming and lonely
      house. From tossing trees
      the torn boughs
hang swaying dislocated, and uneasily
      the wood fire gutters
      as hisses and spits
      of rain sputter and drip
      into tiny blazes. I watch
      the year turning
      and burning to ash
      once more, once more
and hear the breathtaking grave-haunting wolf
      of death at the door.

Poems of Places and People Faber & Faber 1981

CHARLES TOMLINSON

The Marl Pits

It was a language of water, light and air
  I sought—to speak myself free of a world
Whose stoic lethargy seemed the one reply
  To horizons and to streets that blocked them back
In a monotone fume, a bloom of grey.
  I found my speech. The years return me
To tell of all that seasoned and imprisoned:
  I breathe familiar, sedimented air
From a landscape of disembowellings, underworlds
  Unearthed among the clay. Digging
The marl, they dug a second nature
  And water, seeping up to fill their pits,
Sheeted them to lakes that wink and shine
  Between tips and steeples, streets and waste
In slow reclaimings, shimmers, balancings,
  As if kindling Eden rescinded its own loss
And words and water came of the same source.

Collected Poems Oxford University Press 1985

JEREMY REED

Air

Rain water brushed from a swift's pointed wings
on to an eyelash or a spider's web
is how I like to think of the exchange

of altitudes, a vibrant resonance
on this gusty day with birds ticking South
through a needle's eye, each propelled in trance

to dare luminous wind-shafts, and one feels
the elasticity of their wing-pull
in the air's simmer—the twitch of their pole

asserting gravity. The earth transfers
their arrowed passing as the aftermath
of hooves. I crouch down low and consider

the one vertical between me and space
that's flying westwards with the Atlantic,
and watch a singular whitewashed lighthouse

bulb on its rock. Out here the pulse of air
tingles with light hexagonals, I see
it transformed into design and colour

such as the intricacies a snowflake
contrives in fashioning its slow descent.
I sense those sharp intangible facets

pass through me, diamonding the light the way
hail flashes on a heated shovel's back,
or a cormorant's sheen glistens with spray

that smokes on its alighting. Sea and sky
in one illimitable rush of blue
open up light worlds, and the tern's shrill cry

untranslatable holds me static here,
given over to such fluidity
I am become a component of air.

By the Fisheries Jonathan Cape 1984

60 TERRY SETCH *Penarth III* 1981
oil and encaustic on canvas

34 PAUL JOYCE
The Whole Negative, Gwent 1977
photograph, silver bromide print

29 JOHN HUBBARD
Wood with Filtered Light 1965
oil on canvas

45 EDWARD MIDDLEDITCH
The River No. 4 1961
charcoal on paper

56 VICTOR PASMORE *The Snowstorm: Spiral Motif in Black and White*
1950–51
oil on canvas

opposite
10 BILL BRANDT *East Sussex Coast*
1953
photograph, silver bromide print

below
25 ROGER HILTON *January 1964, Red*
1964
oil on canvas

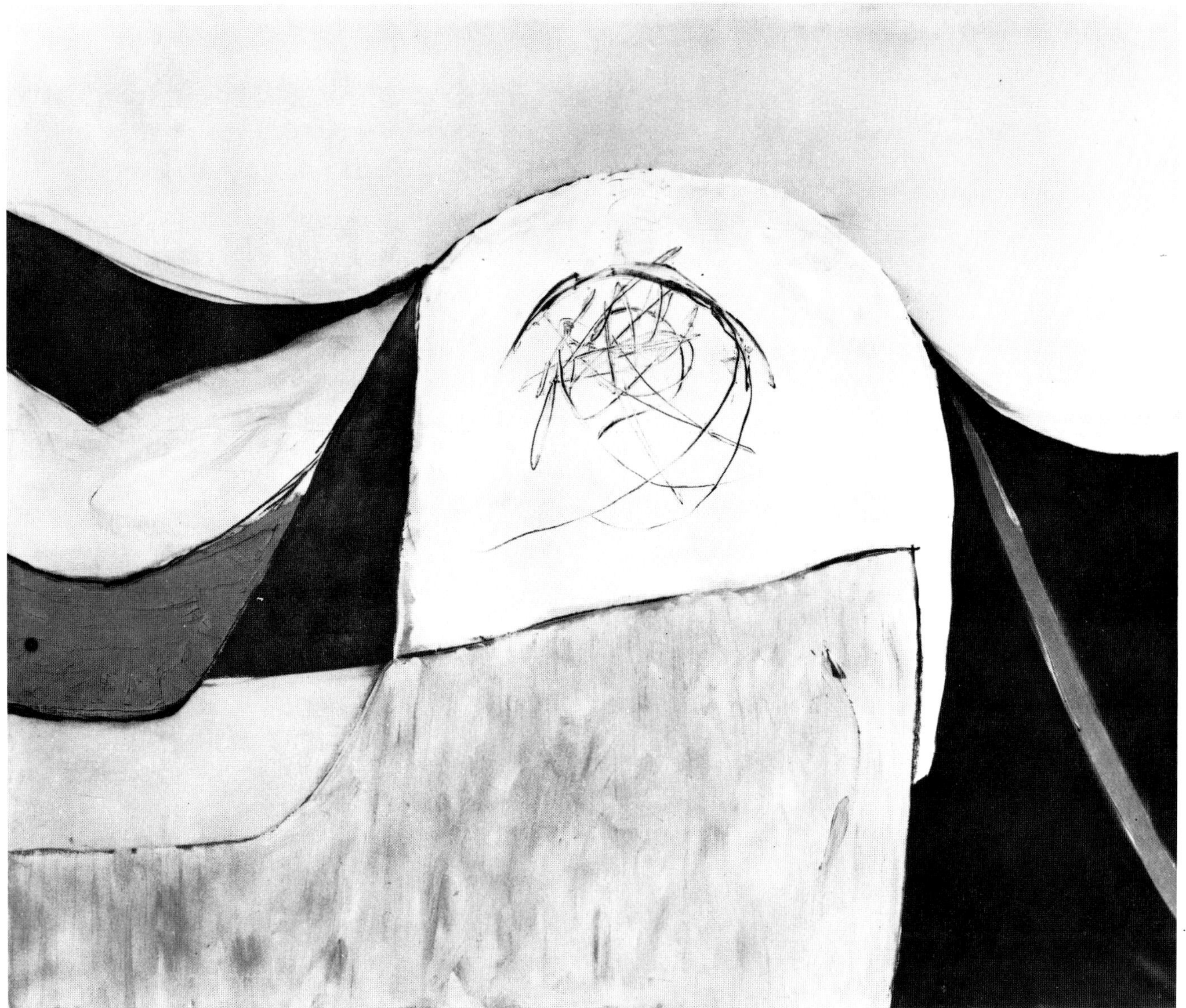

33 PAUL JOYCE *Mountain Road near Rhayder* 1976
photograph, silver bromide print

59 WILLIAM SCOTT
Slagheap Landscape 1953
oil on canvas

58 PETER PRENDERGAST
Bethesda Quarry at Evening 1975
charcoal and chalk on paper

37 JOHN LATHAM *Carberry Bing 1976 Documentation* 1976
photographic enlargements mounted on blockboard plus shelf with aerial view and material from bing in jar

Catalogue

Measurements are given in centimetres, height before width.

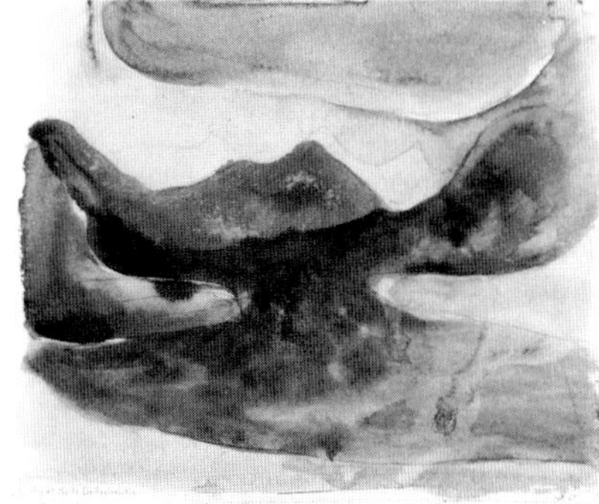
1

● **NORMAN ADAMS**
born London 1927

Adams, now Keeper of the Royal Academy Schools, lives and works in Yorkshire. In 1963 he visited the Hebrides where he later bought a shieling.

'You can't draw the wind; the energy of the sun. It's not just the actual movement of the sea but its energy. And this sense of space. On Scarp you get this extraordinary kind of stereophonic sound at times . . . two different sounds overlapping each other—this sound coming back across the sea, the sea on the rocks and caves—and, in the foreground, this soft and gentle swishing. The mixture of this kind of sound gives one an incredibly vivid sense of space.' (Interview: *Aspects* no. 3, Summer 1978.)

1 **Study at North Ballachulish,** 1965
watercolour and pencil on paper, 20.3 × 24.8

2 **Study of the Sun–Evening, Staffin Bay, Skye,** 1965
watercolour and pencil on paper, 20.6 × 24.8

● **LEONARD APPELBEE**
born London 1914

Studied at Goldsmith's College and the Royal College of Art. Painted Ashby's Barn near Meadle, Buckinghamshire while staying with John Nash (brother of Paul). Lives and works in Devon.

3 **Barns in a Field,** 1940
oil on canvas, 50 × 60

● **FRANK AUERBACH**
born Berlin 1931

Came to London in 1947. Studied at the Borough Polytechnic, 1947–8, under Bomberg. Paints portraits, figures and urban landscapes, all in the studio. Has painted Primrose Hill, north of Regent's Park, since the late 1950s.

'I've got certain attachments to people and places, and it seems to me simply to be less worthwhile to record things to which I'm less attached, since I known about things that nobody else knows about'. (Interview: Arts Council catalogue, 1978.)

4 **Primrose Hill, Summer Sunshine,** 1964
oil on board, 102.5 × 152

● **WILHELMINA BARNS-GRAHAM**
born St Andrews 1912

Having studied at Edinburgh College of Art, moved in 1940 to St Ives to work near Nicholson and Hepworth. 1948–52 visited Switzerland, made studies of glaciers. Wrote in 1965 of a 1950 painting:

'At Grindelwald I was climbing on the two glaciers 'upper' and 'lower'. The massive strength and size of the glaciers, the fantastic shapes, the contrast of solidity and transparency, the many reflected colours in strong light . . . This likeness to glass and transparency, combined with solid rough ridges made me wish to combine in a work all angles at once, from above, through, and all round, as a bird flies, a total experience'.

5 **Grindelwald Glacier,** 1950
oil on canvas, 50 × 76

● **ELINOR BELLINGHAM-SMITH**
born London 1906

Studied at the Slade. Married the painter Rodrigo Moynihan, 1931. Lives and works in Suffolk.

6 **Winter Afternoon,** 1952
oil on canvas, 50.8 × 61

● **DAVID BOMBERG**
born Birmingham, of Polish-Jewish parents, 1890, died 1957

Brought up in London. 1911–13, attended Sickert's evening classes at the Westminster School of Art. Visited Paris with Epstein, 1913, meeting

Picasso and others. Developed a geometric, abstracted style, in parallel with the Vorticists but by 1920 had retreated from British artistic life. 1923–7, worked in Palestine, painting detailed topographical compositions but also more freely handled oil sketches. Travelled widely. 1934–5, Spain. 1945–53, taught at Borough Polytechnic; students included Auerbach. 1947, Summer in Cornwall, painted Trendrine Hill, south-west of St Ives.

7 **Trendrine, Cornwall,** 1947
oil on canvas, 81.3 × 106.7

• **MARK BOYLE**
born Glasgow 1934 and
JOAN HILLS born Edinburgh

Have worked together since 1958 and more recently with their two children as Boyle Family, choosing sites by various random processes and making exact translations of areas of the earth's surface—'Trying to remove the prejudices that the conditioning of our upbringing and culture impose. Trying to make the best visual description our senses and minds can achieve of a random sample of the reality that surrounds us'. They have worked on 'lorry parks, pavements, beaches, a mews, cliffs, quarries, ploughed fields, roofs and many others. On all of these we used some degree of randomness in selecting the actual square or rectangle to be used. We use random techniques to ensure a degree of objectivity.'

8 **Bonfire Study,** 1976
coal, burnt wood, stones, ash and scorched earth
on fibreglass, 182 × 182

• **BILL BRANDT**
born London 1904, died 1983

Spent important formative years in Paris where he worked with the Surrealist photographer Man Ray. From 1945 he moved away from photo-journalism and experimented with nude photography using an old wooden Kodak police camera with a wide-angle lens focused on infinity, a pin-hole aperture and no shutter.

'"The lens", he says, "produced anatomical images and shapes which my eyes had never observed.... It taught me how to use acute distortion to convey the weight of a body or the lightness of a movement." That camera taught him to see more intensely, to perceive in every object the image of another. And the displaced fragments of the female form became the metamorphosed elements of new imaginary landscapes.' (Aaron Scharf: introduction to Arts Council catalogue, 1970)

9 **Pilgrims' Way, Kent,** 1950
photograph, silver bromide print,
35 × 28.5

10 **East Sussex Coast,** 1953
photograph, silver bromide print,
30 × 25

• **ROBERT COLQUHOUN**
born Kilmarnock 1914, died 1962

Studied at Glasgow School of Art 1953–8; met Robert MacBryde. 1941, moved from Ayrshire to London, having been invalided out of the army. Shared studio with MacBryde and, from 1943, with John Minton. From 1943 concentrated on figure subjects. Bryan Robertson described his early landscapes: 'The scene is analysed: its constituent parts separated, annotated, and then packed tightly together again in a new synthesis of inter-locking shapes... The attack had commenced because even in these early works a sharp sensibility and an urge to re-make, to re-articulate the subject were beginning to show themselves. A little later plants or natural forms were detached from the landscape and thrust into the foreground of the paintings, almost as personages in their own right'. (Preface to catalogue of 1958 Whitechapel Art Gallery exhibition.)

11 **Church Lench,** 1942
oil on canvas, 50.8 × 60.5

• **THOMAS JOSHUA COOPER**
born San Francisco 1946

Came to Britain in 1973; resident in Scotland since 1982.

'These pictures are concerned with myths and rituals—stories—of the land and with those who inhabit it.... Native North American, early American pioneer, British Celtic, early Anglo-Industrial Age, and Australian Aboriginal stories and sites have infused the making of this work.' (From Cooper's introduction to *Between Dark and Dark*, Graeme Murray, Edinburgh, 1985)

12 **Ritual Indication, Nesscliffe, Shropshire,** 1974
photograph, gelatin silver print,
19.8 × 29.3

• **JOHN A DAVIES**
born Sedgefield, Co. Durham, 1949

First visited Ireland on an Arts Council award in 1976 and has made several subsequent visits. Commissioned in 1983 to photograph the Canadian landscape.

'I get wrapped up in the speedy type of social existence—which I enjoy—but I also enjoy the barren areas which have not been landscaped by farming or whatever. I enjoy the idea of walking out in fresh air. For me it is exploration. I go to places I don't know, although I have gone back to places. It doesn't matter what the weather is like. I like the variety of changing weather—storm clouds and sun.' (From an interview with James Clement)

13 **Maghera Strand, County Donegal,** 1977
photograph, gelatin silver print,
18 × 27.7

14 **Wicklow Mountains, Wicklow,** 1981
photograph, gelatin silver print,
24.5 × 36

• **JOAN EARDLEY**
born Sussex 1921, died 1963

1939, moved to Scotland and enrolled at Glasgow School of Art. 1950, discovered the Kincardineshire coast and later bought a house in Catterline, a tiny fishing village south of Stonehaven. *A Field of Oats* was painted in the last autumn of her life.

'I find that the more I know a place or the more I know a particular spot, the more I find to paint. I very often find that I take my paints to a certain place, begin to paint there, and perhaps by the end of the summer I have not moved from that place. In fact I have worn a kind of mark in the ground—there is no grass left. I just leave my paints there overnight and eventually a studio seems to have arrived outside. I might just turn round in the middle of a painting and see something else and run back and get another canvas and try to do that, but it is still the same spot really, the same feeling that I am trying to grasp'.

15 **A Field of Oats,** 1962
oil on board, 100.2 × 96.7

• **SHEILA FELL**
born Cumbria 1931, died 1979

'My main concern is landscape (although I have painted several portraits) and I have mostly drawn and painted in Cumbria, Yorkshire and Wales. The chief influence has therefore been that of the country and the different activities which take place on the land, the presence of the mountains, moors, sea and the effect of the changing light in relation to the earth'.

16 **Woman in the Snow,** 1955
oil on canvas, 76.2 × 101.6

• **HAMISH FULTON**
born London 1946

Studied at St Martin's School of Art and the Royal College of Art. More interested in the Oriental landscape tradition than in Western landscape painting. In 1971 he began to make long walks, most frequently by himself, taking photographs en route. Normally a single image is chosen to symbolise the walk. Some photographs have included the signs of man's measure of the landscape such as milestones. Here seven sticks have been gathered and laid to mark the seven days of the walk. Text and photographs are of equal importance.

17 **Seven Days Alberta,** 1978
sepia toned photograph and letraset text on card, 93.6 × 122.6

• **MICHAEL FUSSELL**
born Southampton 1927, died 1974

Lived and worked in Aldeburgh on the Suffolk coast.

'Fussell is dealing with the sea and the weather almost all the time—and the sea is in his weather pictures and the weather in his sea pictures. He is dealing in emotions, situations, feelings about the sea, usually in its darkest and most introspective moods, and about the air, rain, cloud about and above it . . . ' (Sylvester Stein 'The Painting of Michael Fussell'. *The Painter and Sculptor* Summer 1958.)

His work later became abstract though still concerned with outer and inner turbulence.

18 **Heavy Rain over a Marsh (Winter Rain),** 1959
charcoal on paper, 69.9 × 76.2

• **W G GILLIES**
born East Lothian 1898, died 1973

Studied at Edinburgh College of Art 1916–17 and 1919–12, and taught there from 1926, soon joined by MacTaggart. 1920s and '30s painted landscapes, largely in watercolour. 'I have always enjoyed weather, always seen landscape pictorially, and I've got immense pleasure from recording swiftly in drawings and watercolours the fugitive, the subtle, and the grand'. 1939, moved to Temple, Mid Lothian to have landscape close to hand. The Eildon Hills are south of Melrose, Borders.

19 **Eildon,** 1949
oil on canvas, 31.8 × 47

• **CHARLES GINNER**
born Cannes 1878, died 1952

Studied in Paris. Settled in London, 1909. Founder member of the Camden Town Group, 1911. Known for his urban subjects but in later years a frequent visitor to Boscastle on the north coast of Cornwall.

20 **Spring Day at Boscastle,** 1943
oil on canvas, 83.8 × 53.3

• **FAY GODWIN**
born Berlin of English parents, 1931

Has collaborated with several authors on books about various regions of Britain. Talks of 'taking pictures *at* a place' as distinct from 'taking pictures *of* a place'. 'People think landscape photography is a very contemplative thing, and it's true I might stand for an hour or even two with my tripod rooted in the same spot, but I'll often be working at breakneck speed because the light's changing so fast.'

'I go back again and again to the same places, taking photographs until I get the shot I'm happy with. It's a compulsion. I become obsessed and can't let go.' (From interviews with Stuart Franklin and Vicky Cosstick)

21 **Snow on desert of Wales,** 1976
photograph, gelatin silver print, 25 × 37.4

22 **Roman Camp, Trawsfynydd,** 1976
photograph, gelatin silver print, 22.8 × 29.4

• **DUNCAN GRANT**
born Invernesshire 1885, died 1978

Studied at Westminster School of Art. From 1911 co-director with Vanessa

Bell of Roger Fry's Omega workshop and developed work as a designer and decorator. 1916 established a rural retreat with Vanessa Bell at Charleston in Sussex in whose garden and from whose windows they both painted many pictures.

23 **The Doorway,** 1929
oil on canvas, 88×77.5

• **PAUL HILL**
born Ludlow 1941

Worked as a reporter and columnist on local newspapers. Has free-lanced as a photographer since 1965. His landscape photographs have dwelt on signs of human intervention—tracks, walks, stiles, farm machinery.

24 **Stone Wall Complex, Under Whitle,** 1981
photograph, gelatin silver print, 46×28.3

• **ROGER HILTON**
born Middlesex 1911, died 1975

After the Slade, spent lengthy periods in Paris in 1931–9. From 1957 he began to spend time in West Cornwall; the figure and landscape increasingly entered his painting which had been almost purely abstract. 'At one time I was one of the most extreme of abstract painters '54 then I vered (*sic*) slightly'. In 1965 he settled permanently at Botallack, near St Just.

25 **January 1964, Red,** 1964
oil on canvas, 126.9×152.4

• **IVON HITCHENS**
born London 1917, died 1979

1922–25, a member of the Seven and Five Society (originally seven painters and five sculptors) with Ben and Winifred Nicholson, Frances Hodgkins, David Jones, Christopher Wood and others. 1940, London home bombed; bought a piece of woodland at Lavington Common, near Petworth in Sussex where he built a house, created a lake and later acquired an orchard. This garden provided his primary landscape subject thereafter. 'He usually opted for a long, horizontal format—'I find a square-shaped painting usually unsatisfactory because the natural flow of the horizontals is checked. The square shape is itself a unit which needs its counterpoint and in the 'time' factor of a square shape it cannot be repeated or echoed in opposition . . . Therefore I often use this long shape'. 'The essence of my theory is that colour is space and space is colour'.

26 **Garden Cove,** 1952–53
oil on canvas, 44×108

• **NICHOLAS HORSFIELD**
born Surrey 1917

1948–56, a regional officer for the Arts Council. 1956–77, lecturer at Liverpool College of Art. For over thirty years has regularly spent long periods in Normandy, painting Dieppe and Le Pollet, the Seine and its tributaries.

27 **River Epte**, 1973
charcoal on paper, 25.5×35

28 **River Epte**, 1974
oil on canvas, 36×43.2

26

31

- **JOHN HUBBARD**
born Connecticut 1931

Moved to England 1960. 'Before 1968, the paintings were concerned chiefly with colours, contours and dramatically shifting elements of the Dorset coast, where I live. The brushwork was broad and vigorous and the imagery evolved spontaneously from the subconscious memory of familiar places'.

29 **Wood with Filtered Light,** 1965
oil on canvas, 172.7 × 203.2

- **JOHN DICKSON INNES**
born Llanelli 1887, died 1914

1908, became friends with Augustus John. 1910, discovered the isolated inn Rhyd-y-Fen, between Bala and Ffestiniog, where he awoke to his first view of Arenig Fawr of which he made several studies and paintings in 1911 under various light and weather conditions. He buried a silver casket of love letters under a cairn on its summit. Painted in Wales with John and Derwent Lees. Winter 1912, painted with Lees near Collioure in the South of France, wandering up into the hills to find large panoramic views of the Pyrenees.

30 **Arenig,** 1911
watercolour on paper, 30.5 × 43.2

31 **The Coast near Collioure,** 1912
pen and ink and pencil on paper, 22.9 × 35.6

- **DAVID JONES**
born Brockley, Kent 1895, died 1974

Attended Sickert's and Meninsky's classes at Westminster School of Art. Became a Catholic in 1921 and during the '20s worked alongside Eric Gill at Ditchling, Capel-y-Ffin and Pigotts. Exhibited with the Seven and Five for five years. Moved to Harrow in late Summer 1947 to recover from a nervous breakdown—'I paint trees from my window. It's part of the curative game . . .'

'We should miss all the quality of his work if we did not see that it is a combination of two enthusiasms, that of the man who is enamoured of the spiritual world and at the same time as much enamoured of the material body in which he must clothe his visions'. (Eric Gill)

32 **Tree Trunks and Shed,** 1948
watercolour and pencil on paper, 60.5 × 47

- **PAUL JOYCE**
born Hampshire 1941

Has worked as a film, theatre and television writer and director.

'The landscape simply *exists*. It has no account of itself, or of ourselves. That for me is its endless attraction. Have you noticed how we are much more concerned about people who ignore us, than those who listen to us with different degrees of intensity? I am obsessed with nature, for it never fails to offer me sublime indifference.'

In the same interview with Jonathan Williams he quotes the Buddhist Chomei's *An Account of my Hut* (1212): '"The flow of the river is ceaseless and its water is never the same. The bubble that floats in the pools now vanishing, now forming, is not of long duration: so in the world are man and his dwellings." This statement exactly reflects my own feelings about man and his relationship to the landscape. My photographs taught me to feel, or, rather, allowed expression for something deeply felt but unexpressed. In retrospect many were taken at moments of quiet crisis, desperation even. Why should I commune with a camera rather than with flesh and blood? Because it is more *solitary*, naturally . . .' (*From Edge to Edge, Photographs of the Welsh Landscape by Paul Joyce*, Lucida, 1983)

33 **Mountain Road near Rhayder,** 1976
photograph, silver bromide print, 14×30.5

34 **The Whole Negative, Gwent,** 1977
photograph, silver bromide print, 22.5×28.7

• **PETER LANYON**
born St Ives 1918, died after a gliding accident 1964

Except for war service lived all his life in West Cornwall. 'I paint very thin, tall, vertical paintings sometimes because I am fond of climbing cliffs, and I find them very tall and thin. It is just a matter of doing paintings that are not visual paintings so much, but are related to some experience'. (Recorded talk, 1963.)

Took up gliding, 1959, primarily to get to know the landscape better.

35 **Moor Cliffe, Kynance,** 1953
oil on board, 129.5×68.6

36 **Soaring Flight,** 1960
oil on canvas, 152.4×152.4

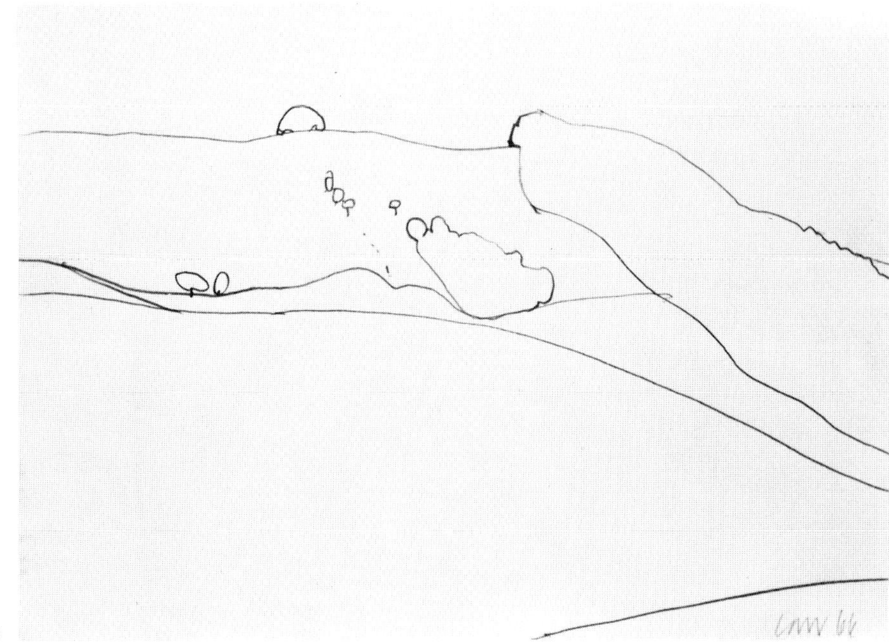

39

• **JOHN LATHAM**
born Mozambique 1921

Formed the Artists' Placement Group in 1966 to place artists in industry. Mid-'70s worked on environmental projects for the City of Glasgow, looking at urban renewal and the problem of slag-heaps. For the tops of trees he proposed erecting 'SKOOB' monuments, based on his earlier burnt book assemblages, and altering public attitudes by photographing them to appear like ancient earthworks.

37 **Carberry Bing 1976 Documentation,** 1976
photographic enlargements mounted on blockboard plus shelf with aerial view and material from bing in jar, 191.9×182.9×25

• **ROBERT LAW**
born London 1934

Self-taught as an artist. 1957, moved to St Ives where he made pots and was encouraged to paint by Lanyon, Ben Nicholson and others. 1959, began to make 'field' drawings, charting his position in time and space and recording his experience lying in fields. These drawings led to abstract 'minimal' paintings. Has read widely: Eastern and Western philosophy, psychology, palaeontology, poetry and, one of his favourite writers, Richard Jefferies.

38 **Landscape Drawing, The White Horse of Uffington,** 1966
pencil on paper, 25.4×35.6

39 **Landscape Drawing, Wiltshire Downs,** 1966
pencil on paper, 25.4×35.6

• **JOHN LESSORE**
born London 1939

1957–61, studied at the Slade. 1978–86, taught at Norwich School of Art. Paints portraits of his family and friends, the neighbourhood of his home in south-east London, and elaborate figure compositions derived from observation of particular places and situations. *La Gardie* is a hill rising above Conques near Carcasonne in south-west France where Lessore has a studio. The hill has now been built on.

40 **La Gardie,** 1964
oil on board, 17.5×21.8

• **L S LOWRY**
born Manchester 1887, died 1976

In his later years Lowry quite often left his home in Mottram to spend two or three weeks away. One of his favourite retreats was the Seaburn

Hotel near Sunderland on the Durham coast. He made several studies of the docks to the south in Sunderland and to the north in South Shields but also made paintings of the view from the hotel. The emptiness of these paintings and some other landscapes is in stark contrast to the animation of his urban scenes.

41 **Seascape,** 1965
oil on panel, 26.7 × 77.8

• **SIR WILLIAM MacTAGGART**
born Midlothian 1903, died 1981

Grandson of the 19th century landscape painter William McTaggart. Deeply impressed by a Rouault exhibition in Paris in 1952. For several years at Christmas the MacTaggarts stayed at Humbie on the Midlothian–East Lothian boundary. The fertile soil of the country north of the Lammermuirs had a special attraction. *Winter Sunset* was probably painted there from nature though from the mid-50s MacTaggart developed a more abstract use of natural themes and moods.

42 **Winter Sunset, the Red Soil,** 1956
oil on canvas, 69.9 × 90.2

• **SARGY MANN**
born Kent 1937

After an engineering apprenticeship, trained at Camberwell School of Art and Crafts. Paints outdoors, normally preferring enclosed spaces. Summers have frequently been spent in Suffolk and Dorset with morning and evening paintings being worked on concurrently. The River Box is a tributary of the Stour in Constable country. This motif was drawn and painted several times and prompted some of his first pictures of this scale.

43 **River Box, evening Sun,** 1981
oil on wood 122 × 152

• **BERNARD MENINSKY**
born Ukraine 1891, died 1950

Brought up in Liverpool. Studied at Liverpool School of Art. Succeeded Sickert as teacher of life drawing at the evening classes of Westminster School of Art. Painted in the south of France, winter 1922–23, and, after illness, in southern Spain, 1935–36.

44 **Andalusian Landscape,** c.1936
oil on canvas, 40.6 × 61

• **EDWARD MIDDLEDITCH**
born Chelmsford 1923

Brought up in Nottinghamshire. After distinguished but deeply disturbing war service, attended the Royal College of Art where he was strongly influenced by John Minton. Exhibited with ‘Kitchen Sink’ artists John Bratby, Jack Smith and Derrick Greaves, but has always been a painter of nature. From the early paintings of *Sheffield Weir* and *Dead Chicken in a Stream* water remained a recurring theme. 1960–61, six months in Andalusia, Spain, a visit from which this drawing probably derives.

45 **The River No. 4,** 1961
charcoal on paper, 69.9 × 99

• **JOHN MINTON**
born Cambridgeshire 1917, died 1957

In an early letter Minton wrote of ‘the touching and melancholy impermanence of all physical beauty’. 1941, worked with Michael Ayrton on costumes and decor for Geilgud’s production of *Macbeth* and in the last year of his life obtained leave of absence from teaching at the Royal College of Art to devote himself to theatre design. Shared a studio with Robert Colquhoun and Robert MacBryde 1943–46.

Sir John Rothenstein wrote:
‘For Minton the example of Palmer was particularly inspiring. Without it, one of his finest works *Surrey Landscape* would hardly be imaginable. It is remote from a slavish imitation: more precise, muscular and altogether crisper than a Palmer, yet it is imbued with much of Palmer’s spirit’. (Catalogue of exhibition, Reading Museum and Art Gallery and Graves Art Gallery, Sheffield, 1974–75)

46 **Surrey Landscape,** 1944
pen and ink and wash on paper, 54.5 × 74.8

• **RAYMOND MOORE**
born Wallasey, Cheshire 1920

1947–50, studied painting at the Royal College of Art. 1956, began to teach photography. Settled in Cumbria in 1978. Many of his photographs are of unpeopled landscapes but showing signs of man’s often inexplicable actions or simply the oddity of the natural—‘the no-man’s land between the real and fantasy—the mystery in the commonplace—the uncommonness of the commonplace.’ (From a 1968 Welsh Arts Council catalogue)

47 **Maryport,** 1977
photograph, gelatin silver print, 21.6 × 32.8

• **DAVID NASH**
born 1945

Since 1967 has lived and made sculptures in Blaenan Ffestiniog (to the east of Innes’s Arenig.)

‘The word ‘tree’ is near to being a verb with a sense of increase, growing, spreading, doing and being; working with plant instinct, transforming raw materials, engaging light, moisture and warmth. There is a presence of evolved wisdom in the success of a tree’s life . . . When no longer a tree each body part contains an imprint of that fluid whole, an echo that gives a sense of origin and nature wisdom. Wood can be worked to retain that echo’.

48

48 **Ash framed with Ash,** 1978
charcoal on paper with ash frame, 69.3×56.6

49 **Larch framed with Larch,** 1978
charcoal on paper with larch frame, 70.1×56.2

● **PAUL NASH**
born London 1889, died 1946

'I turned to landscape not for the landscape sake but for the "things behind"'.

Night Landscape was first exhibited as *The Archer:* the expunged figure is still just visible.

His discovery of Avebury in 1933 proved to be a turning point. 'Their colouring and pattern, their patina of garden lichen, all enhanced their strange forms and mystical significance. Thereafter, I hunted stones by the seashore, on the downs, in the furrows.' At Uffington, he remarked, 'the landscape asserts itself with all the force of its triumphant fusion of natural and artificial design.'

50 **Night Landscape,** 1912–14
watercolour and ink on paper, 37×30

51 **Nest of Wild Stones,** 1937
watercolour and pencil on paper, 37.1×55

52 **Dead Tree, Romney Marsh,** c.1933
three photographs, modern gelatin silver prints,
30.4×55.5, 30.4×18.6, 17.7×30.4

53 **The White Horse, Uffington, Berkshire,** c.1937
photograph, modern gelatin silver print, 23×38

● **WINIFRED NICHOLSON**
born Oxford 1893, died 1981

Married Ben Nicholson in 1920. They met Christopher Wood in 1926, painting with him in Cumberland and Cornwall. A member of the Seven and Five Group, 1923–35. Ben Nicholson lived apart from the family from 1931. Winifred returned to Cumberland at the outbreak of war and, after a period of abstraction in the '30s, resumed landscape painting. The poet Kathleen Raine, a friend from 1948, has said of her flower paintings:

'They were painted with the imagination and not with the scientific eye. The flowers communicated a whole atmosphere . . . they told about places, about the light on a certain day . . . They were focuses for something total which came into every painting [which] was more than the flowers . . . you didn't just look at the flowers, you received a whole atmosphere, meaning, quality'. (From an interview by Judith Collins, quoted in the Tate Gallery catalogue, *Winifred Nicholson,* 1987)

54 **Cumberland Hills,** 1948
oil on wood, 47×45.5

● **VICTOR PASMORE**
born Chelsham, Surrey, 1908

1934, began experimenting with abstract forms. 1937, with Claude Rogers and William Coldstream, a founder-director of the Euston Road School of Drawing and Painting. 1942, moved to Chiswick Mall and in the '40s painted river and other urban landscape subjects, at first influenced by Whistler and Impressionism but, later, more by the spatial construction of Cézanne and Japanese art. He shared Constable's and Turner's love of the transient aspects of nature. 1948, reverted to abstraction. Drawings of the Cornish coast in the early 1950s explore rhythmic, spiral motifs which relate to his interest in Japanese art.

55 **Riverside Gardens, Hammersmith,** c. 1944
oil on canvas, 45.7×61

56 **The Snowstorm: Spiral Motif in Black and White,** 1950–51
oil on canvas, 119.4×152.4

● **MARY POTTER**
born 1900, died 1981

Member of the Seven and Five Group for two years. Moved to Aldeburgh in Suffolk in 1951. 1957, sold the Red House to Benjamin Britten and Peter Pears, moved into a seafront house until a house and studio were built in her former garden.

57 **Sun on the Beach,** 1961
oil on canvas, 82.5 × 92.7

● **PETER PRENDERGAST**
born South Wales 1946

The son of a miner. Trained at the Slade. From 1968 has lived in Bethesda, a small village in North Wales, set at the foot of a huge slate quarry. 'I always work as near to home as I can. I can't see the point of cycling fifty miles to find a subject. . . . There's two hundred years of work in Penrhyn quarry. It had to mean something . . . I went again and again to one spot. I kept trying to draw it but I couldn't make it work spatially. The truth was I had to get back, to draw the whole quarry. It took me three years to realise.' (From *The Road to Bethesda*, Mostyn Art Gallery, 1982)

58 **Bethesda Quarry at Evening,** 1975
charcoal and chalk on paper,
48.4 × 70.4

● **WILLIAM SCOTT**
born Greenock, Scotland, 1913

Trained at Belfast School of Art and the Royal Academy. Before the war stayed for six months in Cornwall, travelled to Italy and lived in Pont Aven in Brittany. In 1950 he wrote: 'During the last ten years I have arrived at expressing my ideas in as direct and simple a manner as possible, taking for my subjects things seen, which are common and ordinary, believing that the poetry of the subject will be in the painting of it.' During the following years he moved away from still-life subjects, introducing figure motifs which sometimes in the course of a painting merged into still life or landscape. He wanted to 'reduce the immediacy of the individual object and to make a synthesis of "objects and space".'

59 **Slagheap Landscape,** 1953
oil on canvas, 71 × 91

● **TERRY SETCH**
born London 1936

Has taught at Cardiff College of Art since 1964, lives and works in Wales. For most of his time he has been preoccupied with the coast at Penarth, immediately outside Cardiff—a beach polluted by oil, strewn with rubbish. A series of paintings, including several large unstretched canvases, derived from the sight of a decaying car wreck. His concern for the environment has recently extended into paintings about Greenham Common. He paints with a combination of oil paint and hot wax.

60 **Penarth III,** 1981
oil and encaustic on canvas, 35 × 40.5

● **SIR MATTHEW SMITH**
born Halifax 1879, died 1959

Studied at the Slade and in Paris. Lived in France, 1908–14. 1920, moved to Cornwall, painted landscapes. 1922, settled in Paris and in 1933 at Aix-en-Provence, thereafter working between London and Provence. Best known for the rich colour and vigorous brushwork of his nudes and still-lifes.

61 **Provençal Landscape,** c.1935
oil on canvas, 25 × 41

● **ELISABETH VELLACOTT**
born Essex 1905

Vellacott recalls memories of nearby woods from childhood years in Highgate. The family moved to Cambridge in 1912 and she has spent most of her life there, her work as an artist extending into textile and theatre design. She began to make sustained landscape drawings outside in 1949 in Llanthony and in the Botanic Gardens at Cambridge. Since 1959 she has lived in a studio house with orchard and garden at Hemingford Grey close to the moated manor house owned by her friend, the writer Lucy Boston. For many years the reproductions pinned up in her studio have included Uccello's *Hunt in the Forest at Night* and an early Mondrian tree drawing.

62 **Winter Trees,** 1969
pencil on paper, 44.1 × 62

● **JOHN VIRTUE**
born 1947

Apart from four years at art school John Virtue has lived in the same area of north-east Lancashire all his life. Worked as a postman. On walks every day he draws in pencil or charcoal, working these drawings up at home with ink mixed with shellac. From 1978, seven years after moving to Green Haworth, he has devoted himself entirely to local landscape and working in ink on paper. Drawings of the same size are moved around until an order is sensed and the group is assembled.

63 **Green Haworth I,** 1979–80
Pencil, charcoal and ink on paper on board,
138 × 104

ANDREW WALTON
born Oxford 1947

Studied at Cardiff College of Art; taught by Terry Setch. For several years he has lived on the outskirts of Oxford responding to the mixture of nature and the man-made. *Garden at Night—Poles* is one of a series of drawings deriving from night walks during an autumn spent in Stithians, Cornwall.

64 **Garden at Night—Poles,** 1982
Charcoal on paper,
80 × 58.2

• **CAREL WEIGHT**
born London 1908

Professor of Painting at the Royal College of Art, 1957–73. Influenced by Munch and, to an extent, by Stanley Spencer, sharing their interest in human situations. His paintings set people, often under stress or involved in mysterious incidents, in landscapes or townscapes derived from real places, attempting 'to get the landscape absolutely right with the people'.

65 **The Good Samaritan,** 1958
oil on canvas, 104.1 × 157.5

• **DERWENT WISE**
born Cleveland 1933

Before leasing a farmhouse in north Northumberland in 1974 Wise worked 'exclusively as a sculptor, but making sculptures with a strong landscape inflection which were informed through landscape drawings. But, living in that landscape for long, uninterrupted periods and fully experiencing it every day, there emerged a strong awareness that the conventions of sculpture were denying the full expression of its particular aspects of mood, light, atmosphere, seasonal changes and so forth—above all the particular sense of place. *Northumbrian Landscape* is one of my earliest essays, still reflecting my sculptural concerns—shape and structure and the demarcation of space; colour and atmosphere are relatively subdued.' He continues to make sculpture.

66 **Northumbrian Landscape,** 1975
acrylic on board, 26.9 × 36.6

• **CHRISTOPHER WOOD**
born Knowsley, near Liverpool 1901, died 1930

Associated with Ben and Winifred Nicholson from 1926, painting with them in Cumberland and Cornwall. Joined the Seven and Five Group. 1928, he and Ben Nicholson discovered the Cornish primitive painter Alfred Wallis but already, in 1922, he had recognised that modern artists were trying to see 'through the eyes of the smallest child who sees nothing except those things which strike him as being the most important'. Leaving Cumberland for Paris in 1928 he wrote to Winifred Nicholson: 'Perhaps I love a life which is not simple and quiet enough for my work. I think I do. The Banks Head life is the painter's life'.

67 **Westmorland Landscape,**
pencil on paper, 27.9 × 38.1

• **BRIAN WYNTER**
born London 1915, died 1975

Moved to Cornwall, first to St Ives, then to Zennor, immediately after the war. 'The Wynter of this period fused an intense feeling for landscape with a cubist vocabulary that was totally literate by Paris standards'. (Patrick Heron) From the mid-'50s he made abstract paintings concerned with flux in nature.

68 **Landscape, Zennor,** 1948
Gouache on canvas, 48.3 × 73.7

Tour

Derby Art Gallery · 11 July to 15 August 1987

Huddersfield Art Gallery · 22 August to 26 September

York City Art Gallery · 3 October to 8 November

Wolverhampton Art Gallery · 14 November to 19 December

Exeter Royal Albert Memorial Museum · 9 January to 6 February 1988

Worcester City Museum and Art Gallery · 20 February to 19 March

Barnsley Cooper Gallery · 26 March to 7 May

Stoke City Museum and Art Gallery · 14 May to 19 June

London Royal Festival Hall · 29 June to 31 July

Walsall Museum and Art Gallery · 6 August to 11 September

Newtown Davies Memorial Gallery · 21 September to 22 October

Ayr Maclaurin Art Gallery · 28 January to 5 March 1989

Stirling Smith Art Gallery · 11 March to 23 April

Wakefield Elizabethan Exhibition Gallery · 29 April to 4 June

further showings to be arranged